Petals of Paper

A Collection

Alexander Lainez

Copyright © 2026 Alexander J Lainez

All rights reserved. This book or any portion thereof may not be reproduced or used in any manner whatsoever without the express written permission of the publisher except for the use of brief quotation in a book review.

Front cover artwork by Alexander Lainez

Printed by IngramSpark in the United States of America.

ISBN: 978-8-9946162-1-5

First printing edition 2026.

Alexander J Lainez
alexander_lainez@outlook.com

Dedication

To Daniel, the Patroclus to my Achilles, thank you for your everlasting love and for always being a reminder for me to love myself as much as I love others.

Thank you to all the people, places, and memories that inspired this collection.

The Ancient Greeks believed in the existence of eight forms of Love.

érōs		page 11
philía		page 19
agápē		page 27
storgē		page 35
manía		page 45
lūdus		page 53
prágma		page 61
philautía		page 69

ἔρως

"*érōs*"

"Romantic, passionate love"

Érōs

With one touch,
a shimmering shiver slithers up my spine.
He leans closer,
looking deep into my eyes
as if to swim in the cerulean basin of my gaze.
Licking his lips,
he leans closer still.
He lingers,
momentarily,
mere inches from my face,
flushed with excitement.

At last, we meet, a merging of two worlds.
The passion of potential promises prompted to purpose.
Perusing the package of phallic pleasure,
Putting orifices of opportunities on other members.

But budding blooms basically lead to bushes of blossoms.
He lay beside me, besotted with belief.
He turns his beautiful visage towards me, as if to speak.

He pauses.

I pray.

He speaks quietly, so that I must move closer,
closer than even mere minutes ago.

"Glory be to Eros who is greatly satisfied.
A pole was erected in her honor,
and she smiles down upon the givers and recipients of flowing waters of love."

In the Pale Blue of Midnight

Under the arch, I wait,
Wondering when it would be my turn to know.
They say knowing is powerful but feeling is everything.
Not only to feel the lightness of longing,
Not only to feel the sensation of seduction,
Not only to feel how gingerly a gentle grazing of lips can turn a whole world upside down.

His hand on mine,
grasping for generations yet to come.
He lowers his gaze to eye my reticent frame
As he couples my cherubness,
Cheekily caressing, carefully.
Catching my breath as he runs his fingers along my spine.
Watching his regard invade my soul,
I shudder.

The pale moon of midnight
Ponders up above,
Partners of Darkness, so we've grown to be called,
Pushing out of closeted doors to break into the openness of nighttime.
Night nears nigh as we say our goodbyes.

With love still lingering on my lips,
My chest glistens with the warmth of action.
I watch him as he slinks away into the folds of my dream.
Forever where he'll stay.

Those who lightly hold love are destined to lose.
But those who let love go, will always win.
But to say "I came, he loved, and I lost"
Is but an admission of longing for a love not to have.

It is within the pale moon of midnight I find my solitude.
Among the fronds of feathered feelings I float.
Flying high above any admonition we may face.
But to say I have lost love but still to have known love,
I will always find my way.

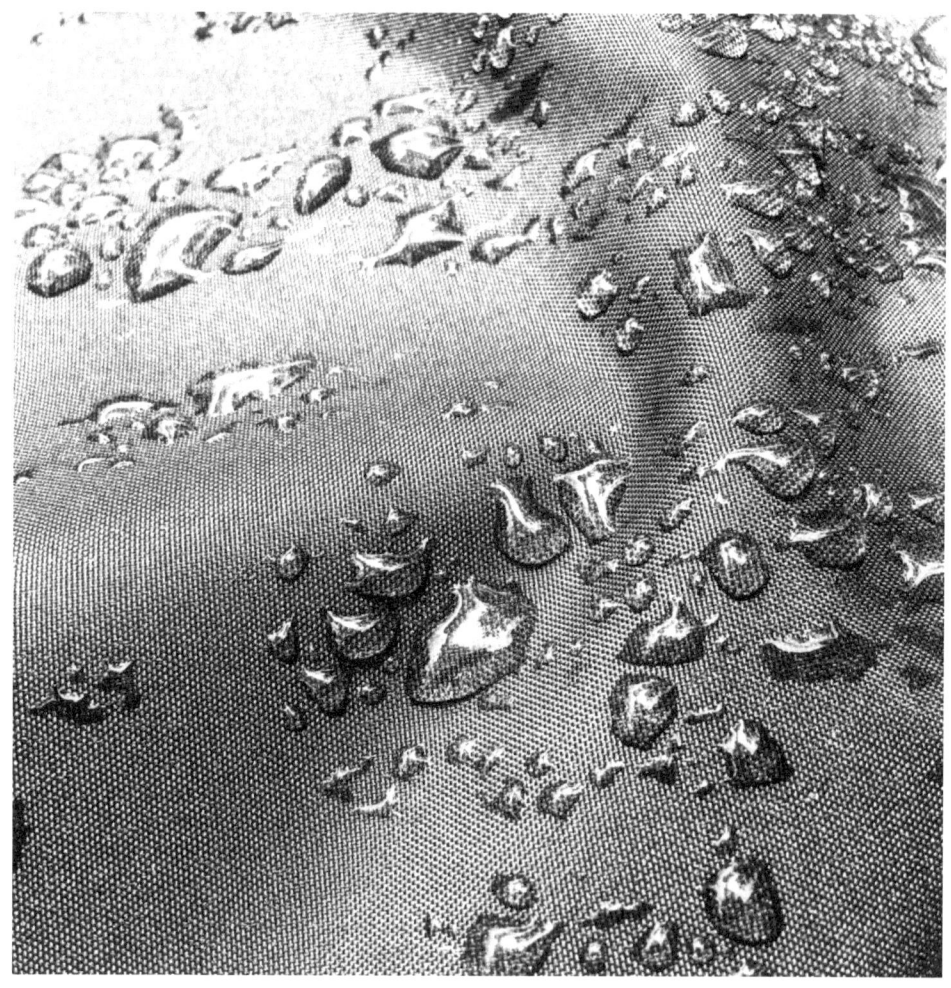

So too, like Dust, I Fall

Minute men-minded minutes of minueted music,
Such as the song of Sirens singing into the gales of summertime,
As Love lays longingly, lit by lighted lips of lusciousness.
His visage varying before me,
bringing my soul into focus as he leans forward.

Oh, but to taste the tenderness of time on his quivering tongue.
Oh, but to utter words mere moments prior to the penetration of his pensive,
Pondering portion of purpose.
Oh, but to speak into oblivion an obligation of ogling of his power.
Power proposes positions prone.

So too, like dust, I fall.

Falling into a love so long-hoped for,
Where others so quickly are able.
To feel but like the liquid from whence life flows.
Relishing the sanguine slice of a sly smile,
Flashing, fruitfully, in front of them.

So too, like dust, I fall.
Climbing towards a summit,
We pause.

Finally, with the wave of work completed,
Exhausted, we lay abutting, breathing deeply.

Φιλία

"philía"

"Affectionate, friendly love"

Philía

Platonic platforms playfully put friendly gazes into focus.
She is like a windowpane through which I find myself.
Grateful for the girl with whom winding worlds right themselves.
Writing words while women like her walk upon this earth,
Seems but a willful attempt to capture the grace she has.

Her face, turned forward,
        beckons the falling moonlight caressing the curvature of her frame.
Her eyes, flashing as cauldrons upon coals,
hold a warmth in them that could melt even the iciest of tundra's with barren hearts.
Her hands, supple and soft, grip the reins of a fate-driven life.
Her voice, silken like honey-dripped dew falls upon a silent pond, sings to welcome
the arrival of a golden mare breaking the dawn of temple-praised goddesses.
Her hair, like tresses of temporal tendrils, is richly dark and delicate as it tumbles
upon her motherly shoulders upon which many have leaned.

Venus-like is she who cradles my heart.
She oft reminds me to focus, freely, finding fortune from within.
The future holds fast the fascinating foundational forces that face me.
She finds, fiercely, time that has yet to slip, suddenly away.
Forge onward towards friendship of fundamental existence
        between one and another.
For it is with her I feel fulfilled.

Philía

Platonic platforms playfully put friendly gazes into focus.
She is like a windowpane through which I find myself.
Grateful for the girl with whom winding worlds right themselves.
Writing words while women like her walk upon this earth,
Seems but a willful attempt to capture the grace she has.

Her face, turned forward,
        beckons the falling moonlight caressing the curvature of her frame.
Her eyes, flashing as cauldrons upon coals,
hold a warmth in them that could melt even the iciest of tundra's with barren hearts.
Her hands, supple and soft, grip the reins of a fate-driven life.
Her voice, silken like honey-dripped dew falls upon a silent pond, sings to welcome
the arrival of a golden mare breaking the dawn of temple-praised goddesses.
Her hair, like tresses of temporal tendrils, is richly dark and delicate as it tumbles
upon her motherly shoulders upon which many have leaned.

Venus-like is she who cradles my heart.
She oft reminds me to focus, freely, finding fortune from within.
The future holds fast the fascinating foundational forces that face me.
She finds, fiercely, time that has yet to slip, suddenly away.
Forge onward towards friendship of fundamental existence
        between one and another.
For it is with her I feel fulfilled.

Amicable Lovers

Close like lovers but distant like two ships passing in the night,
We love each other.
Drawn to each other like moths drawn towards open flame,
We regard each other with pride,
Watching the days since meeting fly by,
as if time was limitless since our meeting was foretold in the stars.
Never did I believe that I,
someone as sardonic and temporally-hardened as a weathered tree,
would meet someone who'd be able to peel back
        layers of cinnamon and pepper-scented bark,
To reveal the honey-soaked sponges of Medovik layers softly sitting beneath.

When in open fields, feeling foolish, frolicking freely,
We meet meticulously, making music made mindfully melodically.
Dreams of ours are boundless and we find our footing amongst the stars.
From the minutes spent rubbing the sleep from our eyes,
To the seconds propping up lids heavy with exhaustion,
We are forging a path forward foretold in the constellations of Plato himself.

A friendship like ours is not uncommon,
Many others understand how it is to enthralled by another.
A kinship, a connection, a bond forged in stone
like the marble masterpieces standing solidly in museums of great art.

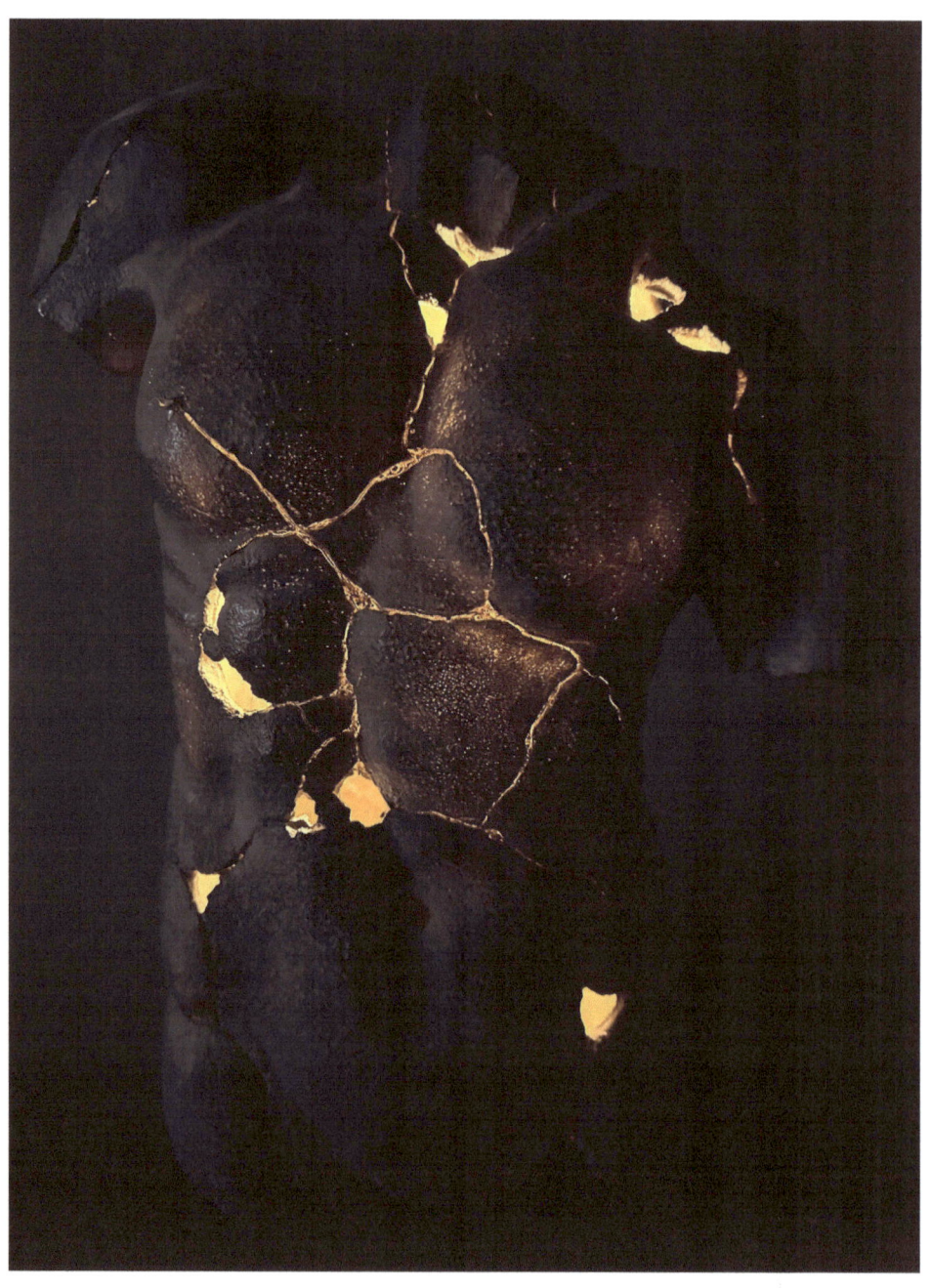

Platonic Passage

With a sincere smile he approaches the bench upon which I'm perched
Like the songbird that sings sweetly the sorrows of the wishes that'll never end.
His words brings the music in my mind to a halt,
He hovers, reading the story written on my face,
He nods as if reading the notes upon the petals of paper that fall to the ground around me.

Our love is never more than platonic,
His hand I'll never hold.
His lips I'll never graze.
But I love him just the same, as he loves me.

I hear my name called out to bring me present to present my gifts of song
Full of words that mask the true love I feel for him.
To be friends with this god-like golden man should be sufficient,
But the succulent shape of his intelligence as it is laid out in front of me
In conversation that keeps me enthralled, ever leaning closer to catch the verbage
He will always be able to capture my attention,
Whether with the stories of his travels of the world,
      (He'll always be more worldly than me
      by nature of his glistening gaze upon the riches of the globe)
Or by his expressions of appreciation of the room we sit in.

The passage of time never feels long because with him I'm home.
I place him on a pedestal so as to let the rays of the sun to catch his heavenly glow,
The Midas touch glistening on his skin,
But I can only wander through the platonic passage.

For his kiss I'll never feel for friendship is the furthest reaches he'll travel with me,
Not that this is a terrible thing, for to be in his life is enough for me,
My love for him sits always on the edge of intimacy,
But he'll never understand that his heartbeat is the one I hear in mine.

ἀγάπη

"*agápē*"

"Selfless, universal love"

Agápē

To love the world,
Albeit the stage that it is,
Is to love the universe within the eyes of another.
The underlying tempo of hums echoing throughout an expansive realm,
Seeming to beckon you forward on a journey towards enlightenment,
Grounds you and pulls you into the lull of laughter and light.
The sun beams overhead bringing a warm breeze across your face,
The gentle kiss of a butterfly brushes strokes of boyish delight
      upon the sun-bronzed beauty of childhood.

To love another as oneself is a tale as old as time.
How often do others love themselves as they want to?
To put oneself forward first finally brings to fruition the fruitfulness of friendship.
Universal truths to be like unbroken golden rods
      laid out beneath the tree of knowledge.
Loveliness of languages whispered wholly upon winds of whim
Reminding of waves of solace,
Silently singing songs of *siempre vivre.*

The world of surrounding rounded corners,
A protection from ourselves
But yet, a reminder of the cruelties of life.
The world reminds us of the promise of tomorrow being not yet so far away.

Panacea

For those who love the world, so limitless in its boundless reach,
May they find the warmth of sunlight spilling over fields,
And hear the quiet hum of rivers winding deep,
Between the hills that cradle forgotten dreams of love and life lost.

For those who love the breeze that stirs the leaves fallen but not forgotten,
Who linger upon the scent of salt on the evening air
        as brine-soaked waves crashing upon a lonesome shore,
Where they gaze upon the stars that flicker against the dark,
Like small fires scattered across the sky.
This is the world of light and darkness they will inherit,
      perhaps only within the dreams of yesterday.

For those who'd love the pulse of crowded streets,
And the way voices blend and drift apart like waves upon ships floating in the ocean
Heading towards the calm corners where time moves slow,
where stillness rests like an old prayer,
Let this be the reality of years to come,
Where forward marching movements meander their way towards a new beginning.

They who love the rain,
Where within the thunder's roar,
Like a lion upon his shore,
who calls out upon the gods with
a voice that is the promise of the storm's release,
that life always finds its way back.

They love the world, in all its chaos and grace,
in moments of joy, in quiet reflection,
for every breath is a gift,
and in each one, they find home.

Alice's Wonderland

Through the looking glass, rose tinted or not, she peers,
Pondering upon the wonders of the world in which she exists.
She lives within the scope of naysayers who view her as a rebel,
But she minds not the simple ways of living they do.

She finds mystery in the flowers speaking to her as she wanders,
Wondering why welcoming the wholly imaginative is so wrong.
She finds inspiration in the caterpillar yet to crystalize,
Absolute acknowledgement of the worlds ability to change,
A hope note yet forgotten by the youthful eyes of a dreamer.

She places a hat upon her head handed to her by the maddest of them all,
Her friend in merriment and mischief,
And turns to face a queen of red, to challenge the Jabberwocky, the champion of none
Slinging a sword of silver over her head as the beast roars.

In its eyes she sees the sadness of so many,
The disinterest in experiencing the love of the universe that she holds so dear.
For a second she hesitates.

All of a sudden, the sadness disappeared and hatred replaced it,
A hatred of all that is unique, curiouser, and real.
The screams of those unlucky enough to be placed in the path of a fire sharpened by distrust of truth
Is heard as the beast screams for the champion of the queen of white.

She is not the wrong Alice as she once stated as she swings the singing blade of variety of views
It connects and slices through the sinewy neck of the beast,
Cutting through the years of stigma, prejudice, and pain,
The head tumbles, seemingly forever, onto the ground,
Coming to a halt at the base of the pedestal of power.

Alice is victorious and, thus, forges forward to share the goodness of openness and tolerance.

στοργή

"*storgē*"

"Familial love"

Storgē

"Birth"

With wide eyes we enter the world
But it is with open arms we welcome our future.
Maternal warmth wraps our wild existence
As if a silken cocoon's spun swiftly, softly, sweetly around our quivering form.
With a cry at our new life, our mother rocks away the darkness
    within which we are found.
Clinging, desperate, we wrench our eyes towards the sky
    but quietly we are stilled by the touch of motherhood.

Doe-like eyes come close,
Closing and opening little windows of water.
A sharp jaw, a face wet with perspiration, drops clinging to a beard yet shaven.
Depth rings out as warm, roughly-soft hands bring us close.
A heartbeat seemingly like our own echoes from within a masculine cavity.
A laugh brings us back into focus as we are made aware
    of more presences awaiting their turn to hold this a new bundle of joy.

"Youth"

Running, quickly, never-slowing, never-stopping we race through time.
We tumble but yet we don't fall.
We hear our parent's call,
But we don't heed.
A Warning.
Don't go, grow, or speak too quick.
Take time to think, breathe, learn how best to approach the challenges of existing.
Be not like the youth of Heraclean notoriety who is brash and impulsive.
Grasp at mere moments of solace and stillness.
A stillness we oft reflect upon as we sit near our parent's knee.
We wish to be young forever.

"Adolescence"

Freedom is what we desire.
Freedom is not yet a figment of celestial existence.
"I want" becomes "I will" with no reflex of admonishment.
The heads shake back and forth, seemingly endlessly trying to hold us
    kept away from our dreams.
"I don't like" becomes "I hate" which we become too comfortable saying.
How little care do we give to people who raised us
    and still love us more than a secondary school doting dashingly dreamy boy.

How soon do we run to the figures of so-called fortresses
        who "don't let us do what we want" when a broken wish
           comes crashing into our lap.
"He said he loved me" we cry as we bury our tear-streaked face
        into a stronger-than-ever shoulder.
Holding us close, as if it were just yesterday we were taking our first breath into crying,
You comfort a troubled heart, broken for the first time, but likely not the last.

"Universal Opportunity"

Separation is not easy.
Too soon the cord of life was cut free from its roots.
The door of delivery closes for what will seem a lifetime.
Windows roll to uncover our parent's faces,
One, trying to be strong, focused on the other who is covered in freedom-granting tears.
She reaches out, grabs tightly ahold of our shaking hand.
Pressing a lifetime of luck into our briny palm.
As the object of delivery rolls away,
A feeling of solitude but new-found universal opportunity washes over us.

"Matrimonial Memory"

An aisle lays before you.
The man of your dreams stands, handsome, smiling,
        wiping tears of joy off his tanned face, awaiting your arrival.
You walk, arm entwined with the wisest of women, towards the entity of a new future.
You reach the end, you turn to your ever-loving mother, who is shedding tears so pure they glisten and gleam like diamonds upon a linen cloth,
        and lay upon her blushed-polished cheek a kiss of gratitude.
You turn and look at your father,
Bemused by gates holding a flood of cherished memories.
His eyes radiate from under his emotion-pained brow
        as he gazes upon you and your future.
His smile, saddened by the reality of this matrimonial memory,
        holds the words you always heard:
           "We love you, Son."

"Terrible Twos"

How quickly are we brought back to reality as the seemingly two-ton-tantrum-tossing child lunges towards tempting times.
Often do we commiserate with our parents who laugh
        and remind us of ourselves at that age.
Little ball of energy, enthusiastic in all forms of learning, looking up at us as we sit
        as soldiers to ensure the safety of our little one.
Our child, giddy with the gumption of grand dreams,
        goes surely through their life as they embrace the possible.

Misunderstood, misheard, or misbehaved, our little one, enamored with their existence,
        expresses themselves without any regard to reticence.
The "terrible twos" are but a reminder of the opportunities for growth and understanding.

"Twilight Years"

As the inevitable creeps closer and closer,
As twilight dawns a new era,
As opportunities will come swiftly for sorrowful serenity,
We prepare.
Preparation is a word as light as a ton of bricks weighing down upon a chest.
To find time to express all that is possible and necessary to be said
        in such a short time is like threading a never ending eye of a needle,
There just doesn't seem to be enough thread left of the spool
        so pulling quickly makes the fated time come faster even still.
Saying goodbye is one thing,
But to help another, much younger, cope with the moment of unknown bliss
        is an act of true love.
To explain the turning of the tides as if life were but on a wave of time
Is simple to say that every person will come to the shoreline at one point or another.

"Final Horizons"

"Goodbye" must be the hardest to say when we know it's for forever.
With such love did our parents love us and with such love did we reciprocate.
To be loved by a parent is an honor indeed,
        but to love a child as a parent had once loved us or even better is a privilege.
To build upon a foundation, however stable,
        to nurture future generations is a task we are given.
Let love be the guiding hand in their journey through life.
Let tolerance and acceptance of others be the very essence upon which their joy is based.
Final horizons are not yet made final.
The sun will shine forth another day.

Paternity

Like a leader of many,
He strides forward carrying the weight upon his broad, mountain-like shoulder.
Stooping, not under the pressure of years of lessons,
But to support one slipping behind.
Joy does he know and proclaim
As many of kin stand facing him.

A love unlike any other
Is that of a father and a son.
A humble rumble stirs from within a heart built by Prometheus
Showing, outwardly, the strength of connection,
Whether by birth or by selection,
Between a Man, ripened by tireless years, and a son, nubile in a world of their own.

To be but the man a father is, was, and ever shall be
To some, may be just a fantasy.
Emulating a representation of manliness,
Yet with softness and grace not unbecoming of a man,
Is to sit across a table and to ask for enlightenment found
        from within a maze of life-informed choices.
Memories flit endlessly between the windows of the soul,
Lighting up a face warmed by an ever-dulling sun.

Lessons learned written upon the arms of a man
        whose folly was to dilly dally among the flowers,
Smell them, we are told, but we often do not.
Lying among the lavender-scented linens lays the frame of a once mighty man.
To say words of admiration and appreciation in memory of one who lived
        for the thought of passing on an Odyssey may seem to be too late,
But to light a flame from within oneself to carry forth the lessons
        taught by he who has fallen into an endless sleep is solace.
Peace is paramount and provided by those whose fate is to ponder.

With pieces of a puzzle does a man become a father and so a child becomes his son.
Like Kipling once wrote, "You'll be a Man, my Son!"

Maternity

Warm waves of wonder wash upon the wandering child within her gaze.
The one who is beholden to the glories of a mother be but a million reasons for affection.
The quick eye and ever-faster reflexes pulling her offspring from the jaws of life,
She surveys the world within which the child will meander,
searching always for an opportunity to steer them along the best path forward.
We oft hear of two roads diverging within a wood but not of the multitude of
municipalities of magnificent mountains that pepper the landscape of a child's life.

The job of a mother is never complete.
She must be ever-cautious while still molding a curious spirit within her child.
She must be ever-vigilant while still engaging the yearning
       for freedom ever-spewing from her child.
She must be ever-loving, especially when providing subtle gestures
       towards opportunities of enrichment to her child.
She must be ever-patient especially when faced
       with the unruly and anxious musings of her growing child.

A mother's love is all-encompassing, never wavering.
She guides the eyes of youthful curiosity as it looks
       upon hills and valleys of lessons yet to be learned.
She cradles the innocence that is her infant.
She pulls close the moments held dear of her toddler.
She reflects fondly on the angers and frustration of her child's innate desire
       to know more, have more and achieve more.
She smiles, remembering how often her child strived for greatness
       in the smallest of moments:
              Their first cries, their first steps, their first words

A mother's love is a testament to taking the world upon herself,
An outward showing of humility and selflessness.
The instances of fear and disappointment nullified
       by moments of celebration and excitement.
Any memory of discomfort and pain healed by the sound of her child's laughter.

To be a mother is to be a caregiver,
       giving care to ensure their child finds their place in life.
To be a mother is to be a nurturer,
Instilling the constant reminder of the strength
       of love and kindness when making decisions.
To be a mother is to be a referee,
Always reminding that mindful actions often involve compromise.

A child, in the eyes of their mother,
Is ever young, ever youthful,
But the day will come when a child becomes an adult in their own right.
The pain of releasing their child, now grown, into the world,
       Is yet another reminder of the often thankless task that can be motherhood.

μανία

"*manía*"

"Obsessive love"

Manía

Darting eyes,
tears drip, dropping down a shaken visage
Desperately deciding the path to choose towards despair.
His affection was all I desired,
All I cared for, and all I'd ever want.
His attention, his intention, his love
Was everything to my whole being.
Without it, I could crumble.

Dependency drives direction
Co-authoring the sentiment of sentences derived from dreams.
These dreams hold deeds done not to me but to the others with whom is heart lies.
He will be mine and mine alone.

Obsession overtly overrides order.
Awkwardness often arranges allowances of others
To allow for poor behavior.
Choose wisely the definitions of details determining deals between parties.

Decidedly viewing through a red-tinged lens, I wait for his approach.
Cloaked in the darkness of a pure ending from which no one can escape.
Hesitation strikes me stricken with solitude
For it is too late.

His lips of everlasting silence hover nearby.
His breath upon my stone-cold brow, furrowed under his reproach.
Lightly do his lips leave his mark upon my marbled expression.
Glassiness glosses over the glazed windows into the soul.
Vacancy takes hold,
And, with one final breath,
I give into the mania of my last moments of life.

Gatsby's Daisy

He thinks of her when the sky is too quiet,
when the wind forgets to speak.
The memory of her voice so clear and sweet like a bell on a crisp morning.
Her face and warm gaze linger in the chasm
        between each haggard, liquor- laden breath,
                a hazy shadow that stretches endlessly across every waking thought.

His soul trembles with the weight of words unsaid,
His strained hands tracing the outline of her very absence
as if the memory of her in his hands could fill the hollow.
Every moment, conscious and unconscious, without her
feels like a ragged wound that will not heal,
a dull ache that deepens with each passing second
like the drop of a weighted ball down within the deepest depths of existence.

He waits, like a panther baiting prey, in the spaces she once filled,
clinging mercilessly to the echoes of bell-like laughter,
the softest brush of her name upon his drums, until it becomes a prayer,
a prayer whispered against the existential dark,
until his world forgets to exist without her in it.

And yet, despite the ever-closing expanse between them,
no matter how lithely she slips silently away,
he cannot and will not stop reaching,
cannot and will not stop wanting.
This Love, a dark, obsessive hunger that fills the cracks,
but never the whole.

With a Glance

His eyes hover, glancing.
I feel the sickening sweet sensation up my spine as his hand travels,
Ever so slowly, towards my bare neck,
Soon to grasp, to wrangle my breath from my throat.

He laughs,
I fall even harder.
I know only his gaze as our eyes meet
As he wipes his essence from my bruised lips.
I tell myself that one day I'll be free from his fortress of fornication,
But, for now, I can only shudder.
I don't know what led me to this gauntlet of love,
If even I can call it that.

He pushes me, hard,
My face against the wall, between the rocks,
And whispers my name,
Constantly fleeing from within the lips of Lucifer.
Never will I escape the taunts
as he tears my vestments from my fragile frame
      as he nears the rear port of forced entry.
Again and again, over and over,
The rhythmic timing of his haggard breaths as he reaches his climax
Is but a constant, consistent catastrophe within which I am caught.

Like a hyena, he laughs.
Licking his lips, proud of his work,
He cleans himself in my hair,
Wiping away the remains of my dignity.
I can feel his devilish grin burning into my back,
Like a cow prod, searing in between my shivering shoulders.

He shoves me away from him,
As he stumbles towards the new morning
And I am left, clutching to the casualty that is my life,
I am alone to face the harshness of sunlight bearing down
      on the now raw rump of reality.

I am in love with the man in my dreams,
Not the figure who manhandles my innocence at every chance he takes.
I claw my way towards my own freedom,
Running away from the only reality I've known.

They say if you tell yourself a lie enough times, you begin to believe it.
But dare I say, I don't just believe it - I live it.

He loves me not and yet I still return.

Lūdus

"*lūdus*"

"Playful love"

Lūdus

Like friends, we hold each other close.
Longingly, lovingly do we regard one another.
Brushing the hair out of his face,
He smiles and grins,
Looking at me as his lips part,
    Allowing words so heavenly linked together to tumble out, "I want you."
His face reddens as he leans back,
Allowing the moonlight to bounce off his glistening chest.

Adonis so is he, as is he, like amber and gold, his body like a temple,
Strong and solid,
Shining like bright diamonds,
His perfect points upon the upper figure,
Gleaming, beckoning for gentle kisses.

His love, his tenderness, stills me.
His hands find their way, needing no guidance.
I lay back, as if in a bed of silken flowers,
And am transported to paradise.

Like lovers, I hold him close.
The friendliness of our embrace harkens, here, to an opportunity in passing.
For once we were but only friends, fellows, now integral partners in life.
Suddenly, as if time itself had ceased to exist,
    as if Kairos himself had perceived its coming, he laughed.
His laugh rang like tiny bells within a modest chamber,
Not as one would chuckle at a farce,
But in glee, celebration, or remembrance of a memory
    of when we had but joked that we'd share this moment.
Swiftly, we joined gazes, and I saw the beauty of his eyes,
Like two beautiful pools of honey,
The bronze sun shone from within his loving look.

I felt, in this pinnacle moment, a sense of peace.
Friendly foolishness fell far from the bedside of two who became one.
Playfully, consummate, did we, our passions for one another.

The Lauded Lad

With what words do I describe this man that haven't been spoken?
The Herculean form, the piercing gaze, the flaxen hair
Are but things that make one swoon, but interest me not.
The witty way wonders of worldly wandering he whispers to me in the dark
Make me wish I were but the tunic flowing around his tight, taut, torso.
But to tell him would only inflate his infallible instincts of my longing for him.

His mother appears always like a woman taking the turn of the tide too far.
She is reluctant and reticent when I am lingering in her presence.
I am inclined to believe that she'd rather see me torn to pieces by wolves
Then see my love for her son.

He, alone, sees me as an equal,
While others are more than prepared to say I am but his friend and companion.
He, alone, can make me not feel inferior to his greatness.
The greatness of his strongly chiseled chin,
The greatness of his powerful python-ed grip as he gathers me
       like a basket of amaryllis.
The greatness of his tongue as it laps up my elixir of passion.
The greatness of his soul that searches my mind for more ways
       to make me melt into loving him.

With great power, he takes me in his arms
As we roll in the throes of the fruitful fruition of our fantasies,
His lips parted, seeking something southern,
Landing on his mark, he smiled.
Shivering silently slowly relishing the moment, I seeded his expectations.

How unprepared,
How unwilling was I,
How little did I know of his fate.
To know that an arrow of another could take from me what was mine.
As he lay in my arms, I wept.
Bitter tears of brined brokenness brought a barren wasteland upon me.
He whispered his last breath, a name, my name,
Patroclus.

And with that, my lauded lad, my love, left me *sine mea Achilli.*

As Two Ships

Bodies of water lay out before us,
Yet, I still see the glimmer in his eyes.
Like two pools of diamonds are the windows into his glorious soul,
        Two pools I see myself swimming around to capture
                the lapis-encrusted gaze of my desired.
His smile is like a beacon across open water,
        Beckoning me to draw closer.
His laugh is like a horn signaling his intention to board.
His strong, yet soft, grip on his helm, guiding into my open port,
        We meet again, at last.

As two ships pass in the night,
We wish to surrender to the waves of passion we feel approaching.
But scared, are we, of making the first move.
Never have we stepped over the threshold
        into one another's sanctuaries,
        we merely have had an affinity.
From a distance, did we regard each other,
Not knowing how to truly proceed.
We loved each other, but could never find the words to express.

In silence, sometimes, we swam together through the charted waters
        laid out before us by society,
We desired for something different, something uniquely ours,
        but yet forbidden by others.
Only gods and goddesses were to be together, never two gods
        (or goddesses, for that matter).
We longed for the opportunity to demonstrate the love we had.

Playing in the crashing waves upon the shoreline,
We frolic, hand in hand, heart to heart,
        tasting the sweet saltiness of the sea.
The sun glimmers upon the ocean as if Persephonē were being born.
Like gemstones being scattered upon the shore, we confessed our love,
        Knowing we couldn't hold out much longer.

Our ships crash upon the shores, hardened by the rocks of time.
Two souls joined together by the intense desire to be one.
With love in our hearts, we finally succumb to our wishes,
And found ourselves charting new territories.

πράγμα

"*prágma*"

"Enduring love"

Prágma

For it to be but a love that grows over time,
It must be rooted in commitment, molded by understanding.
It is not within the passion of first meetings,
A lover's fleeting, often unremarkable, embrace,
but upon a stalwart foundation, built upon the joint effort of two hearts.

This love blooms and prospers within compromise,
where both hearts and minds give and negotiate the world within their story,
with the understanding that this truly is how the union endures.
Patience but becomes the tongue of connection,
tolerance the space in which it can take on new and exciting forms.

Through opportunities of growth, the enduring foundation doesn't break.
Rather, the love learns, it amplifies,
an evolving covenant that refuses to languish.
This true love, ripened and matured,
is not fleeting, but steadfast—
an enduring promise to exist as equals for a lifetime.

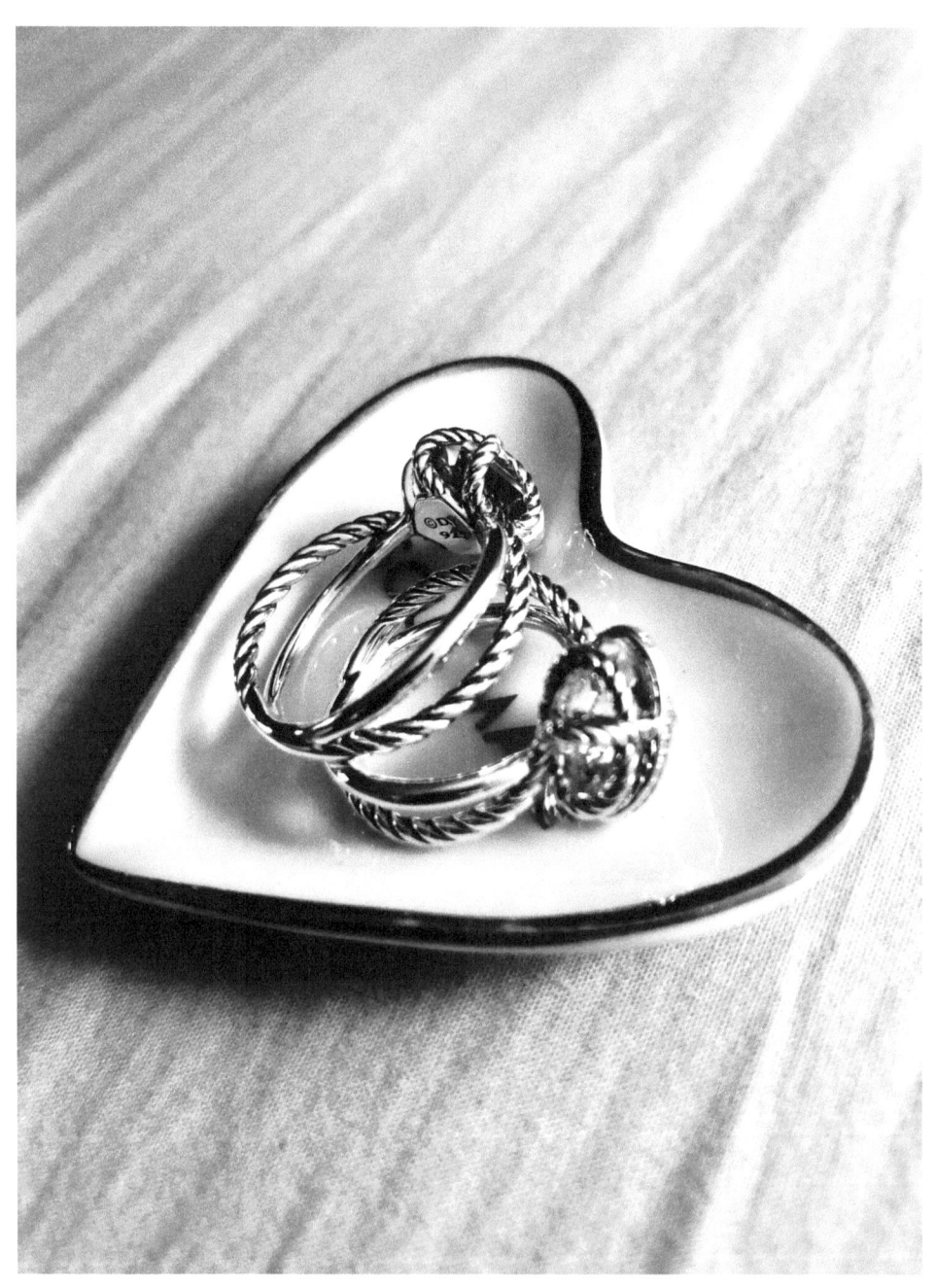

What He and I Chose

Our story didn't start with sparks or declarations cried into night air.
It began in a quiet whisper—
in the breath before the confirmation,
in the alcove where listening waits.

Two young lovers,
Like Patroclus and Achilles
Sitting back to back,
With heads tilted upon strong shoulders,
not longing for halves
but presenting whole selves,
Exhausted of pretending
that queer love must be dramatic to be real.

There is no swiftness here,
only a heartbeat-like return
To the promise that doesn't always untangle,
to the hands and embrace that hold without wanting to fix.

We are not always patient —
but we are invested.
To rebuilding,
to growing with,
not against.

Love, for my Patroclus and me,
is not a dramatic flourish.
It is a lush garden.
No longer needing to be Secret.
Some moments we forget to water it,
sometimes it blossoms without effort.
But always, like Patroclus forever returns to Achilles,
we return.

We do not ever pledge never to stumble—
only that we will stand up again, together.
That we will take care of what matters
even when it is not convenient to us,
Especially, even, when it is not easy.

This is what we and so many chose:
not the Achillean lore,
but the making.
Not the ideal match,
but the practice.

Not just love — but life, shared.
Forever and Always.

Forever and Always

With love, all is possible.
I look at him, the Adonis among the others,
The person with whom I'll spend the rest of my life,
The person who lifts me up when I am down,
The person with whom I brace against the storms of life,
Never faltering, never shying away,
Never denying that the foundation upon which we stand
       has been built over years of agreements, compromises, and discord.
It is through his eyes that I see a world where two became one
Where so often the odds are not in our favor.
Our love, not unlike so many others, is unique in its challenges,
But we rise to the occasion, confirming our commitment.

I'll love you, forever and always,
Like the ever-turning, ever-spinning of the planets in your eyes.
Like the warmth found only within your embrace.
Like the security steadfastly solid within your stance upon the earth.
Like the ringing of light bells when you laugh.
Like the promise of eternal, ever-lasting love found within your heart.

I'll cherish you, forever and always,
Especially in the moments when the world feels like too much,
     and my thoughts have a mind of their own,
          you remind me of the calm.
Especially in the moments where the light behind my eyes has been diminished
     and I find difficulty in locating joy,
         You center me and remind me of the honesty that lives
             in those moments and push me to create my own happiness.

My love, my gorgeous man, my everything.
It is with you all is possible.
It is with you all my days will be spent.
    Forever and always.

φιλαυτία

"*philautía*"

"Self love"

Through the Eye of the Needle

Standing in front of a community that loves only those who look to thread a needle
Isn't easy to do with a head held high,
Pondering lofty ambitions of searching for a knight in shining armour
      who is beholden to a man others often pass by.
A man grossly figured (per snide letters lining an orange-masked approach to
connect) left behind with the other unwanted, undesired.

It is difficult to love what is staring back in the mirror.
Abomination knows but one word - Self.
It is unlikely that someone who is told that their worth is not unlike refuse left beside
a receptacle would be able to face themselves with a positive-singed delicacy.

High praises are not sung by a community seemingly built upon inclusive beliefs.
Inclusion only includes idols of Adonis-like figures,
      effeminately-thinned spectators, and those gifted with rods of creation.
Fuller-figured are only deemed worthy
      by those who expressly chase such opportunities.
'Tis a chance that those fattened by the Fates are doomed to take up space that
seldom others wish to be in.

Philosophical faults fall firmly fast
Among attendees attempting to add
To tides of temporal tenures, tapping, totally, towards termination.
It is patronizing when those better lotted in life belabor the importance of philautia.
Thread comes in a multitude of sizes, only some will thread life's needle.
Force it and the eye will break.

Broken like the dreams of wedded fantasies
      dashed upon jagged walls closing in to cut those down to size.
Broken like uncomfortable visits to rooms of mirrored attempts to pull sewn fabrics
of the world across a mannequin that is padded beyond common dimensions.
Broken like the beads of sweat-laced drops
      cascading forward down headed towards earth.

Unbroken is the belief of worthlessness,
Wholly and honestly held,
As Helios hold his gilded reins rounding the Golden disk of light.
Rounded, fattened by the sweet succor
      of successful munching of bountiful feasts laid out by Dionysus,
Prepared for slaughter, sent into the
Labyrinth to be game for Thesus's victim.
The only godlike-figure destined for those
      who thread not the eye of the needle is that of the slain Cyclops,
Killed by their own stupidity.

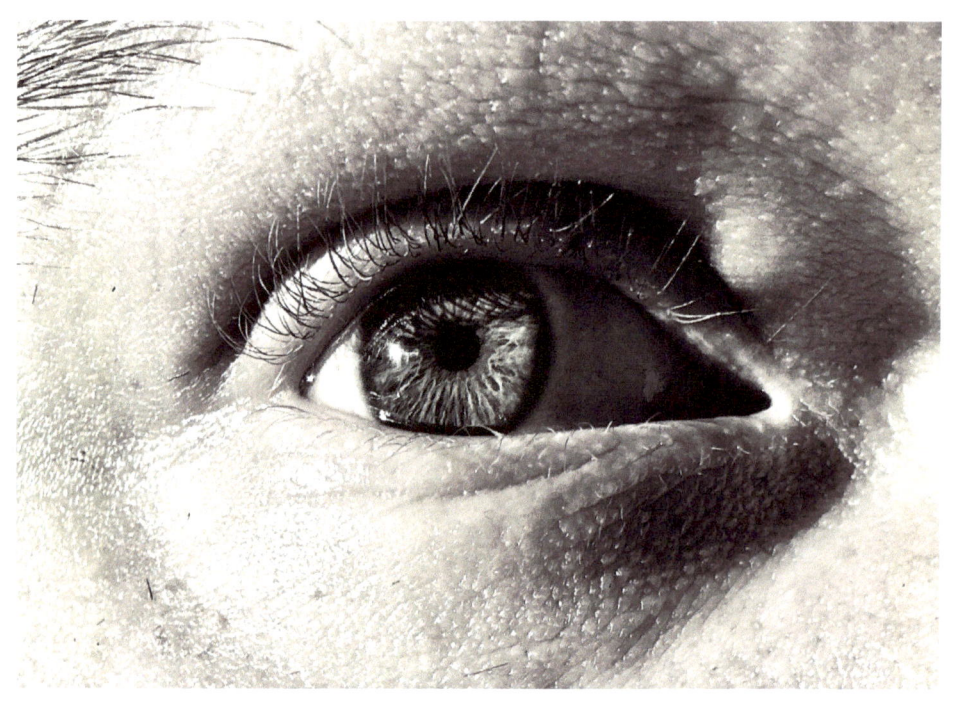

Love Thyself

To love thyself is to find strength in the places
        where the world doesn't demand any different,
and your heart can rest without fear of judgment.
To be yourself,
even in moments of stillness,
To encapsulate an existence within a breath,
To allow yourself to dream even when the world turns its gaze elsewhere,
and you feel the cold weight of Time's hand upon your heart.

I speak, quietly, into the expanse of the universe with great pride,
a whispered affirmation that I belong in a world often set against me.
I allow myself to touch my own skin,
For once not with shame,
        but with a reverence as if an Adonis were sat in front of me,
Tracing along the scars,
a history of the opportunity to find love
that's always been mine to claim.
Each mark, a story of resilience only I know.
Every curve, Time's testimony to growth.

I no longer need to seek the affirmation
of false pretenses who cannot accept me as whole individual,
To love thyself is learning and striving instead to trust
the patterns of your own heart,
the quiet reminder,
you are worthy.

And in those moments, often few and far between,
when the noise of a cruel world fades to oblivion,
I can smile,
not because I am happy in that moment,
but because I have finally learned how to love the man I have always been.

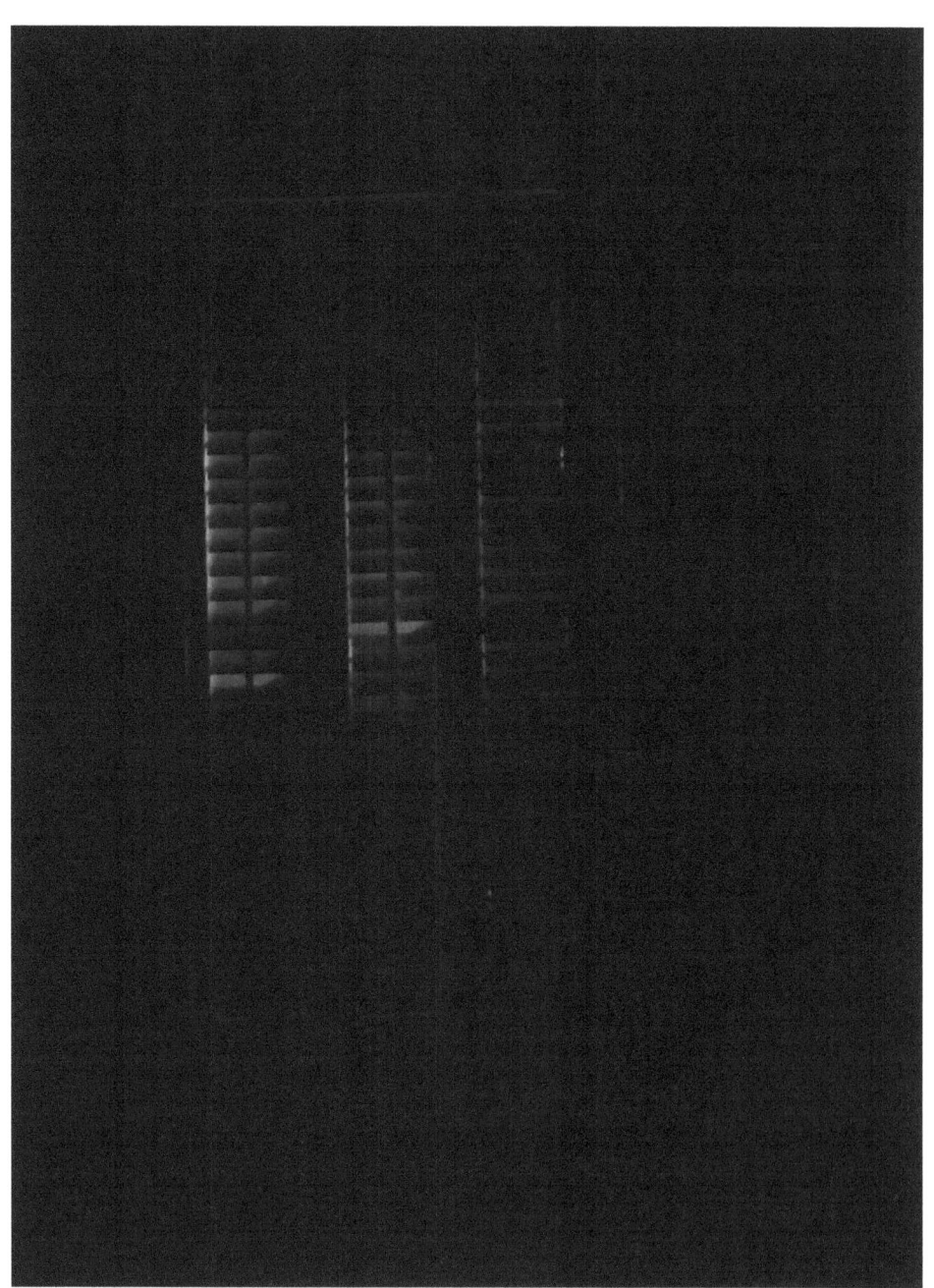

When One Closes, Another Opens

Blink, and it'll be gone.
The image of worthiness not determined by others,
As fleeting as it may be,
It is possible.

Blink, and the world will go rushing by like a torrent of rain,
Water wiping wandering wondering and wishes away.
Wishes of a beautiful tomorrow,
Dreaming of an image to behold,
    with a lithe smile,
    but like an even thinner thread of hope.

Beauty does not need to lie beneath a surface smoothed by ripping winds,
Beauty does not need to be curated like art within a monolithic statue repository.
Beauty can function in ways unbeknownst to those who search tirelessly.
Beauty can be more that what meets the naked eye.

They say beauty is in the eye of the beholder,
But how often than not do the eyes of another cast shadows of doubt?
When one set of eyes closes, another is beset upon the true nature of love.
When one window into the soul becomes secluded into sinews of a lidded cap,
    Windows into the dimension beyond are opened.

Look upon oneself,
Not with judgement for so many others have set out to do such a thing,
But with love and compassion for the soft, underbellied creature that stands before.

About the Author

Alexander Lainez is a poet whose work explores varies themes common in day-to-day life while still emphasizing the importance of the small moments. His poetry is known for its raw, honest exploration of the human condition and focuses on the celebration of how intimacy between people is rooted in love for one another.

Alexander began writing poetry at a young age, drawing inspiration from the people and experiences around him. He seeks to encourage people to look at their life from different perspectives and hopes that his work is a tool that can break down barriers that stand in the way of open dialogue.

When not writing, Alexander enjoys designing and creating floral arrangements, finding new Pug and Brussels Griffon accounts to follow on TitkTok and Instagram, and searching for his favorite non-chain coffee shop with his husband, and muse, Daniel.